Citizenship

Following Rules

Cassie Mayer

Heinemann Library
Chicago, Illinois

Designed by Joanna Hinton-Malivoire
Illustrated by Mark Beech
Printed and bound in China by South China Printing Co. Ltd.

11 10 09 08 07
10 9 8 7 6 5 4 3 2 1

The Library of Congress has cataloged the first edition of this book as follows:
Mayer, Cassie.
 Following rules / Cassie Mayer.
    p. cm. -- (Citizenship)
 Includes bibliographical references and index.
 ISBN 978-1-4034-9487-0 (hc) -- ISBN 978-1-4034-9495-5 (pbk.)
 1. Obedience--Juvenile literature. I. Title.
 BJ1459.M39 2007
 179'.9--dc22
                         2006039385

Contents

Following rules means doing
things the right way.

Following rules makes it fair
for everyone.

When you raise your hand
before speaking ...

you are following the rules.

When you ask before taking something ...

you are following the rules.

When you wait for the
teacher's instructions …

you are following the rules.

When you ask before doing
something ...

you are following the rules.

When you walk down the
hallway ...

you are following the rules.

When you play safe ...

you are following the rules.

When you listen to what someone
tells you ...

you are following the rules.

Following rules is important.

How do you follow the rules?

Activity

How are these children
following the rules?

6148

Picture Glossary

fair agreeable for everyone

Index

Note to Parents and Teachers
Each book in this series shows examples of behavior that demonstrate good citizenship. Take time to discuss each illustration and ask children to identify what would happen if people did not follow the rules. Use the question on page 21 to ask students how they can follow rules in their own lives.

The text has been chosen with the advice of a literacy expert to enable beginning readers success while reading independently or with moderate support. You can support children's nonfiction literacy skills by helping them use the table of contents, picture glossary, and index.